Uproar a[...]
funerals, [...]
hand in hand.

This new collection on grave
moments, from the author of
Tombstone Humour, recalls lighthearted
past and present events to do with
death and burial.

GRAVE MOMENTS

or
Dead But Hardly Buried

RICHARD DE'ATH

London
UNWIN PAPERBACKS
Boston   Sydney

First published by Unwin Paperbacks. A
division of Unwin Hyman Ltd, 1986

UNWIN ® PAPERBACKS
40 Museum Street, London WC1A 1LU, UK

Unwin Paperbacks
Park Lane, Hemel Hempstead, Herts
HP2 4TE, UK

George Allen & Unwin Australia Pty Ltd.,
8 Napier Street, North Sydney, NSW 2060,
Australia

Unwin Paperbacks with the Port Nicholson
Press
PO Box 11-838 Wellington, New Zealand

© Richard De'ath 1986

**British Library Cataloguing in Publication
Data**
De'ath, Richard
    Grave moments, or, Dead but hardly
    buried.
    1. Death — Anecdotes, facetiae, satire, etc.
    2. Funeral rites and ceremonies —
    Anecdotes, facetiae, satire, etc. I. Title
    393 GN485.5

    ISBN 0-04-827143-8

Typeset by Computerised Typesetting
Services Ltd, London N12
Printed in Great Britain
by Cox and Wyman Ltd, Reading

For
JACO GROOT
The Flying Dutchman
– with thanks

CONTENTS

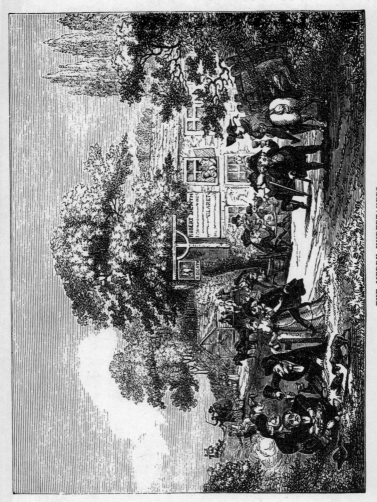

THE MERRY UNDERTAKERS.

PREFACE

For a number of years I have had a copy of a sketch, made towards the end of the eighteenth century, called 'The Merry Undertakers'. It caught my fancy originally because it happens to mention a forebear of mine, Robert Death, who was the owner of a popular tavern called 'The Falcon' located in London at the corner of the Wandsworth Road, leading towards Battersea Bridge.

In those days, the inn stood among trees and it was obviously a haven much used by travellers in and out of the capital. Contemporary accounts also say that Robert Death was a man 'whose figure ill comported with his name, seeing that it displayed the highest appearance of jollity and good condition'. No doubt the good Robert was at his best the day the artist of

the picture, 'a merry-hearted fellow named John Nixon', passed by, for Nixon was evidently much amused at the sight of a company of undertakers enjoying themselves at 'Death's Door' – as the same account amusingly puts it – and promptly captured the scene for posterity.

There is also a reference to this picture in Robert Chambers' famous *Book of Days* (1863) which, when I came across it some years ago, provided the germ of the idea for the collection of grave moments gathered here. Let me quote for you Chambers' description of 'The Merry Undertakers':

> Having just discharged their duty to a rich nabob in a neighbouring cemetery, they had, the first time for three or four hours, found an opportunity of refreshing exhausted nature; and well did they ply the joyful work before them. The artist, tickled at

a festivity among such characters in such a place, sketched them on the spot, and his sketch was soon after published, accompanied with a cantata from another hand, of no great merit, in which Sable, the foreman of the company, is represented as singing as follows, to the tune of 'I've kissed and I've prattled with fifty fair maids':

Dukes, lords, have I buried, and
    squires of fame,
  And people of every degree;
But of all the fine jobs that came in my
    way,
  A funeral like this for me.
    This is the job
    That fills the fob,
O! the burying a nabob for me!

Unfeather the hearse, put the pall in
    the bag,
  Give the horses some oats and some
    hay;
Drink to our next merry meeting and
    quakery's increase,
  With three times three and hurrah!

Chambers ends his account with what seems like a touch of regret. 'Death has now submitted to his mighty namesake,' he says of my ancestor, 'and the very place where the merry undertakers regaled themselves can scarce be distinguished among the spreading streets which now occupy this part of the environs of the metropolis.'

I've often thought how I would like to have joined old Robert and drunk along with him and his buryin' friends. But if such a thing is impossible, I can at least keep his spirit alive by showing that uproar and undertakers, fun and funerals, chuckles and cemeteries still go hand in hand, and though you might imagine that most things to do with death and burial are invariably grim, you'll learn very much to the contrary in the pages which follow.

Nor are the grave moments of

which I speak merely things of the past. Any business which can currently boast a man named 'Colonel Cinders' (in California, naturally!) who performs the last rites for more than 14,000 people a year – and members of the dear departed who have recently asked to be laid to rest in tombs shaped like a minaret, a piano and even a sports car, can hardly be said to be entirely without humour!

If anybody typified the idea that there could be something to laugh about in a graveyard it was Joseph Grimaldi (1779–1837), the world's most famous clown who was renowned for his performance as the cemetery night-watchman. His memoirs, edited by Charles Dickens, show time and time again that though death is the last taboo, he thought we ought to try to laugh at it!

I'm glad that the memorial service

for Grimaldi featuring a congregation of clowns in full motley is still held each year, and after years of neglect the site of a demolished church in Islington where he is buried is to become a memorial park in his honour. He is one person who would have been delighted at the idea of people walking all over his grave. He'd be even more amused at the fact that the headstone which once adorned his grave now languishes in a shed used by a workman, just like the one he immortalised a century and a half ago!

For Joseph Grimaldi – and I hope for you, the reader – grave moments like these are to be savoured and enjoyed.

Richard De'ath
February 1986

I

GRAVE WORK
Undertakers' Accounts

An Irish undertaker on the scene of a
railway accident in County Cork, in
1906, was reported to have told the
two assistants who came with him to
'get the dead and the dying into
coffins as quickly as possible'.

When one of the men pointed out
that some of the victims were alive
and might be saved, the man retorted
sharply, 'Oh, bedad, if you were to
pay any attention to what *they* say, not
one of them would allow that he was
dead!'

Retired doctor Omar Philips of
Oklahoma was a fastidious man who
had carefully arranged every aspect of
his life right from his youth. He
carried this attention to detail up to
the very moment of his death.

For prior to committing suicide
with a shotgun in August 1938, he
calmly telephoned a local funeral
parlour and reported his imminent
death – as well as giving instructions
for his funeral!

*   *   *

Undertakers have been given some
strange instructions in the last wishes
of their customers – but few have
been more amusing than those made
by Tom Bedford of Poole, in Dorset,
in 1949.

He asked for his coffin to be stopped on its journey to the cemetery outside his favourite local pub and there left for an hour while his friends had a few drinks at his expense.

'And before the undertaker leaves the pub,' Tom instructed, 'I request that he pours a beer over my coffin, too.'

*　　　*　　　*

A Colchester, Essex undertaker found himself with some curious instructions when he was preparing the body of Arthur Smithson for burial, in 1958.

Mr Smithson had for years nursed a fear of being buried alive, and therefore requested that one or more of his toes or fingers be cut off in the mortuary before he was laid in his

18

coffin, 'in order to ensure that I am
dead'!

$*$ $*$ $*$

Headline from the *Scarborough Evening
Post* of 16 July 1958:

UNDERTAKER'S FAILURE
Let Down By Customers

$*$ $*$ $*$

The following report was carried by
the *Daily Telegraph* in August 1960:

19

'Guests at Mr Henry Allen's barbecues in the garden of his house at Milford, New Jersey were upset by the sight of coffins being carried into the adjoining undertaker's premises.

'Mr Allen complained to the town council, which yesterday ordered the undertakers to erect a barrier of trees.'

*   *   *

It was the most embarrassing moment the undertaker in Miami, Florida had ever encountered.

A much respected local citizen had died in May 1966, and a spacious tomb complete with inscribed memorial stone had been ordered and duly erected before the funeral.

It was just moments before the mourners were due to arrive at the cemetery when a horrified assistant pointed out to the firm the terrible mistake that the stonemason had made on the memorial stone.

For in the last name of A. Perfect Whitt the W had become an S . . .

*   *   *

It was more like a scene from the Wild West than a funeral when the cortège of a rich Italian was shattered by a fusillade of shots which peppered one of the finest hearses in Naples, as it carried the man to his last rest in March 1967.

The incident occurred at Casal di Principe, north of Naples, and was

the result of the man's four children deciding to see their father buried in splendour. They approached various undertakers and selected a Neapolitan firm because of its impressive hearse drawn by six, black-plumed horses.

All went well until the funeral party was on the way to the cemetery – when shots rang out from behind a hedge. At this the coachman in his long black coat and top hat leapt down from the hearse and fled across the fields.

Police regarded the act as being the work of a rival firm of undertakers, jealous at having work taken from them in their territory.

* * *

One of the most curious deaths on record must be that of a reclusive and obviously mean undertaker named Osbert James Gardner of Wisconsin, USA who was found frozen to death in bed, in December 1968.

Mr Gardner, who was 91 and had only retired from the family morticians business the previous year, had ordered the heating to be cut off from his home a few days beforehand because he considered the fuel bill exorbitant.

And yet in a coffin which he had had built years before in preparation for his own death and which he kept beside his bed was found . . . over $200,000 in crisp bank notes!

*　　　*　　　*

The bizzare scheme of some German undertakers to recycle coffins came to light during a court case in Dortmund, West Germany, in October 1976.

Before the court were Herr Gerd Fasta and two employees of the Dortmund Municipal Crematorium. Giving evidence against them, Herr Johannes Wassah and his wife.

Said Frau Mathilde Wassah, 'Had it not been for the deaths of two relatives within six months we would never have suspected Herr Fasta, our family undertaker, of being involved in theft.'

To which her husband, Johannes, added, 'Because we were not that close, we bought my Uncle Kurt an oak coffin that had been reduced because of scratching. When we had to cremate his stepsister a few months later we were offered the same coffin, now stained mahogany, as new. But I recognised the scratches.'

The court was told that it had been discovered that by using the lid of one coffin with the base of another, the accused were able to save one complete coffin from every two cremations.

Passing jail sentences, the judge commented, 'The thieves had recycled more than 500 coffins before they were caught. Their procedure yielded enough ash to allay the suspicions of the bereaved.'

*   *   *

After years of working as a mortuary assistant in New Orleans and never being given an increase in his salary, Jason Connor began systematically to steal small sums of money from his employers.

By the autumn of 1977, he had
amassed over $2,000 which he kept
hidden in his toolbox awaiting the
opportunity to sneak it out of the
building.

But when Jason's employers
noticed that money was going missing
and instituted a sudden spot-check of
the mortuary, he had to stuff his ill-
gotten gains hastily into one of the
coffins. *There* he believed it would be
safe until after the search, when he
could retrieve it.

Unfortunately, before he could
carry out his plan the coffin went off
for cremation . . .

*　　　*　　　*

Undertakers have had to accept being
the target of jokes for many
generations now.

But in 1977 two irate undertakers in Brighton really thought the owner of a new shop sandwiched between their premises had gone too far when she put up her sign. And so they promptly lodged a formal appeal against her planning application.

But were *their* faces red when they learned what the shop was really going to be used for – a beauty salon. And the name?

The Body Shop.

*   *   *

A course in 'Death Education' which consisted of visits to graveyards, mortuaries, embalming parlours, as well as lectures by experts such as priests and undertakers, was

organised by Mr James Speaker of Ohio, USA, in the spring of 1978.

Hoping to decrease the natural anxiety felt by many people about what he called this 'taboo subject', Mr Speaker also invented a way of measuring established attitudes towards death – on the FOD (Fear of Death) and DA (Death Anxiety) scales.

'Our aim,' he explained, 'was to modify existing reactions to these natural facts. We used a control group to check our results – which were dramatic.

'All our students became more fearful and more anxious as a result of the course,' he said. 'Those measured on the DA scale were less affected than those on the FOD. But we are making progress. Very soon we shall know how to find a consistent Fear and Anxiety Reversal Programme!'

Some years ago, a Surrey mortuary was so busy that a member of the staff with a rather macabre sense of humour posted the following notice on the door:

STANDING ROOM ONLY

The man was promptly dismissed.

*　　　*　　　*

The story of 'Speedy' Atkins and his undertaker friend, A. Z. Hamock, became famous all over America in 1980. It happened after 'Speedy' made his first appearance on TV – fifty-two years *after* his death!

'Speedy' was a much respected man in his home town of Paducah, Kentucky, who tragically fell into the

local river and drowned in 1928. The body was passed into the care of his friend the undertaker, A. Z. Hamock, who out of affection decided to embalm 'Speedy' before laying him to rest in the local cemetery.

By a curious twist of fate, the same river that had drowned 'Speedy' flooded nine years later and brought his coffin back to the surface. In the battered casket, the little man was found 'looking as good as new' to quote his wife, Velma.

Because of this, it was decided 'Speedy' should go on show in the funeral parlour. And when A. Z. died in 1949, the business was taken over by Velma Atkins.

Hearing this story in November 1980, the producers of the nationwide TV show, 'That's Incredible', decided to feature 'Speedy' Atkins.

'When they asked for him to appear on television, I dressed him up in a

tuxedo and we got right on the jet,'
explained Mrs Atkins.

After making his debut, 'Speedy'
became an overnight star – the talk of
America. Commented one of the
show's organisers, John Caldwell,
'A.Z. did a great job, for "Speedy"
looked like he was still alive – apart
from the fact that his skin was like
wood.

'In fact, he was a lot more lively
than some other guests we've had!'

*　　　*　　　*

In 1980, an American widow, Mrs
Marjorie Toller, announced that she
was suing the Plantagenet Casket
Company of Michigan for $5 million.

Explaining her case, she said, 'In
the middle of my late husband's

funeral I suffered a heart attack. The
pall-bearers were loading his casket
into the hearse when the bottom
dropped out and a body that was not
my husband's fell on to the road.

'In addition to this strange body,
the coffin was stuffed with copies of
Playboy magazine, a huge bundle of
panty-hose, and about two dozen
Coca-Cola cans. Everyone burst out
laughing,' she added.

*   *   *

The Grim Reaper was a guest at a
party held near Kuala Lumpur, in
January 1981. When the supply of
spirits ran out, the revellers began
drinking a home-made concoction
called 'Samu'.

One by one guests collapsed in a stupor, and it was only when the host tried to revive a party-goer and suspected that the man was dead, that it was realised a tragedy had occurred.

And, indeed, before medical assistance could be summoned, no fewer than twenty-eight of the guests died.

In a later report of the party it was said that all the guests had been . . . undertakers.

*   *   *

Story from the *Eastern Daily Press* of March 4 1981:

People are being overcharged on funeral costs, the Lord Mayor of

Norwich, Mr Ralph Roe, told the
city's health committee yesterday.

'Some people are being taken for a
ride by funeral directors,' Mr Roe
commented.

*   *   *

Mr George Paulos' night out at
Castleton House in Dublin, at
Christmas 1981, was suddenly
interrupted around midnight by a
request that someone wanted to speak
to him outside. Mr Paulos, an airline
manager, who had been looking
forward to the evening and had even
hired a special dress suit from some
Dublin outfitters, went rather
reluctantly to the door.

The man waiting to speak to him
proved to be an undertaker.

34

'I am sorry to interrupt your evening,' the sombre figure said, 'but I have a contract with the outfitters and I need that suit you're wearing to dress a corpse that is being buried in the morning at ten o'clock. You see it's the only one the shop has in stock that would fit the dead man!'

The somewhat startled Mr Paulos was told by the undertaker that he had brought a plain suit as a replacement – and still rather dazed the airline manager went off to give up his suit for a dead man!

* * *

When Mr Charles Schiller of Boston, USA was made redundant by the firm of undertakers he worked for in 1983,

he was given what at first sight seemed an unusual parting gift.

But not so, according to Mr Schiller.

'My leaving present of two elm coffins, with brass fitments, may seem ironic,' he said, 'but this is not the case. I have always wanted to set up on my own, and this is the ideal opportunity.'

*   *   *

An American safety-on-the-roads campaign, in 1983, made use of the image of the hearse to drive home its message.

To combat drunken driving, it was announced that a series of roadside signs were to be erected across the country. The first of these read:

'Drinking drivers, nothing worse
They put the quart before the
hearse!'

*   *   *

With the introduction, in 1983, of
letters of the alphabet before the
numbers on the registration plates of
motor vehicles, a London undertaker
found the plates on his hearse became
grimly appropriate the following year.
 Previously, his registration had
read 111 URN – but in 1984 when he
purchased a new hearse and
transferred the old plates, it became
B 111 URN.

A pitched battle was fought during a
funeral in the black township of
Soweto in South Africa, in April 1984,
according to a report in the *Rand
Daily Mail*.

The paper said that nine people
were stabbed in the battle which was
caused by rival undertakers clashing.
The incident was later blamed on
'business jealousy'.

*   *   *

Two hearse drivers were dismissed by
a firm of funeral directors in Cardiff
after a number of fiascos, according to
a report in *The Times* of September
1984.

These funeral fiascos included a
fight between the two men outside the
church during a funeral service, and

putting topless pin-up pictures in a garage where priests parked.

On another occasion, one of the men went to work in training shoes and white socks, and at a funeral stood in church beside a coffin combing his hair. Both men also refused to go out on a call until they had finished their fish and chip lunch.

According to *The Times*, the men dropped their claim for unfair dismissal when an industrial tribunal was told of their record.

*   *   *

Advertisement from the 'Situations Vacant' column of the *Daily Telegraph* of 29 January 1985, placed by a firm of funeral directors in Orpington, Kent:

DUE TO BEREAVEMENTS we have vacancies for funeral directors. For further details of our salaries, free medical insurance, and death in service benefit, please contact . . .

*　　*　　*

According to a report in *Paris Match*, in March 1985, there have been some unseemly scenes in the French capital in recent months with rival hearses battling for possession of bodies. This has resulted from a declaration that a 1904 bill which gave local authorities exclusive undertaking rights was illegal.

'In the latest incident earlier this month,' the paper reported, 'the Gaullist mayor of a Paris suburb prevented the porters of an

undertaker with anti-Gaullist
sympathies from carrying a coffin into
a church in his district. The mourners
had to bury the body themselves.'

*   *   *

Three masked gunmen made a grave
mistake when they decided to rob a
crematorium in Enfield, Middlesex, in
April 1985.

The men burst into the Enfield
Crematorium and tied up the twenty
members of staff while they waited for
a security van to deliver the wages.

But the bungling bandits didn't
know that the security firm had
switched their delivery time until six
hours later – and after a frustrating

wait of an hour the men went off empty-handed.

'Their big plans were left in ashes,' a police spokesman said later.

*　　*　　*

An undertaker bought forty-four coffins which had been stolen from a rival for the bargain price of £10 each, according to a report in *The Times* of 19 April 1985.

Appearing before Marylebone Magistrates Court, James Shackleton was said to have told the police he knew the coffins were stolen, but the price was 'too good to pass up'.

Shackleton told the court the coffins were used for 'low class funerals'.

'There is a lot of rivalry in the funeral business,' the undertaker said, adding that he was out of work because his hearse was damaged and off the road.

*   *   *

Enterprising mortician, Danny Morley, opened the Family First Casket Outlet, a coffin shop between a discount store and a tanning parlour in a Missouri shopping centre in September 1985, according to a report in the American press.

His prices, he said, were half those charged by funeral contractors and he hoped to turn his burial outfitters into a national chain.

On offer in the Family First Casket Outlet were coffins ranging from a full

ceremonial walnut-with-brass model
at $1,060 to a cloth-covered
cardboard casket at just $50!

*   *   *

'A grave-digger was turned into a
public relations officer overnight by
Left-wing councillors in Liverpool
and told to preach Militant doctrines,
it was revealed yesterday' – from the
Daily Mail, 6 November 1985.

*   *   *

'Dead Right' might be the most apt
comment on this report from the *St
Albans Observer* of 5 December 1985:

'The mortuary at St Albans City Hospital is an unhealthy place to be, St Albans councillors heard last week.'

*　　*　　*

Oh, the irony of it!

A report from Jakarta, in January 1986, reported that an Indonesian MP had died in a road accident on his way home after winning a two-day battle in the regional Assembly to secure funds for an item urgently needed by a local city hospital.

The item? A hearse.

*　　*　　*

The very latest thing in the death business in America is the drive-in funeral parlour, according to a report from *US Today* magazine of January 1986.

The first of these buildings has been opened in Los Angeles (where else?) and a special feature are the see-through plastic coffins which enable relatives to view their deceased without even having to get out of their cars.

*   *   *

There was a shock in store for residents of Morningside in Edinburgh, Scotland, in February 1986, when they awoke one morning to find this sign unfortunately erected

46

outside the premises of the local undertaker:

'Do not attempt to enter box until your exit is clear.'

*   *   *

There have been some singularly appropriate names for undertakers over the years. Take, for example:

DEATH & SONS
of Bildeston, Suffolk

WAKE & PAINE
of Twickenham, Middlesex

Mr BONES
of Glasgow, Scotland

WILL PLANT
of Swansea, Wales

J. POSTHUMUS
of Grand Rapids, Michigan

GOODY P. CREEP
of Salem, Massachusetts

and perhaps the most notable of all:

GROANER DIGGER
of Houston, Texas.

*   *   *

And just a few more suitable names
for the record:
   In America there are funeral
businesses called **THE MOLE
FUNERAL HOME** in Georgia and

THE QUICK-PARK FUNERAL
PARLOUR in Ohio. Canada has
THE WING ON FUNERAL HOME
in Toronto, while South Africa has
HUMAN & FITT FUNERAL
SERVICES in Pretoria.

In Britain, the National Association
of Master Masons meet at
TOMBLAND in Norwich, Norfolk,
while the Secretary of the National
Association of Funeral Directors is
called RAY HEAVEN.

II

GRAVE EVENTS
Funeral Tales

There are few odder funerals on record than that staged by the Roman poet, Virgil, who spent almost £50,000 burying a *fly*!

The funeral took place at Virgil's town house on the Esquiline Hill in Rome, and was carried out with 'barbaric splendour' to quote one report. There were also funeral orations read by other famous poets, before the fly was laid to rest in Virgil's grounds.

But there was method in the poet's seeming madness. For a decree had been passed in the Second Triumvirate that the lands of the rich could be confiscated to be given as reward to returning war veterans. The only exemption was land in which someone near and dear was buried – and Virgil claimed his immunity on the basis of his pet fly!

*   *   *

Passions were certainly not buried along with the corpse of the famous French poet, Paul Verlaine (1844–96), when his funeral took place in Paris, in January 1896.

No sooner had the graveside service been concluded, than a fierce struggle

developed between the poet's publisher and his mistress for possession of the dead man's winding-sheet.

And while this disturbance was going on, a light-fingered member of the congregation named Louis Ai stole away with fourteen of the mourners' umbrellas which had been left leaning against a tree while the coffin was lowered into the ground!

*　　　*　　　*

Oscar Wilde (1854–1900) delighted in telling the story of the fellow countryman he saw watching a funeral in a rural district of Ireland.

'Is that a funeral?' he enquired of the man.

'Yes, sir, I'm thinking that it is.'
'Is it anybody of distinction,' Wilde added.
'I reckon it is, sir.'
'And who is it that died?'
'The gentleman in the coffin, sir,' came the rustic's reply.

*   *   *

Extract from the 'Vicar's Notes' in the parish magazine of All Saints' Church, Manchester, in 1936:

'I shall be away from the parish attending the Diocesan Clergy School from 21–24 April. It will be convenient if parishioners will abstain from arranging to be buried, or from making other calls on me during this time.'

It was a moment to savour for 88-year-old Mr Wade Millman of Coatsville, Indiana, when he stood up to preach at a funeral service in June 1937 – *his own*!

Over 500 people packed the town's little church – with over 5,000 more outside – to hear Mr Millman declare, 'There never has been such an occasion as this in the world. Columbus wanted to preach his own sermon. So did Napoleon and Napoleon's wife, but they didn't. I am.'

The service was complete with coffin, pall-bearers and a specially carved tombstone ordered from Switzerland. Mr Millman apologised for delivering his address without a collar or tie, 'but I haven't been able to find one since my wife died'.

He said that he had lived a moderately good life, and had never worried about things, 'because

54

worrying makes you roll over and wear out the bedclothes'.

Mr Millman added that the only thing he was sorry about was that his horse, John, aged 36, was not present in the church to hear his address — but he had been frightened away by all the people and traffic outside!

*   *   *

Knowing only too well the old saying, 'You can't take it with you', wealthy Joaquin Felinna, of Vila Boim in Portugal, decided to have the last word on his relatives whom he suspected would squander his hard-earned cash.

And so, in May 1942, as he lay on his death-bed, Joaquin mustered all his strength, gathered together his

banknotes in a pile, and ceremonially burned them.

The ashes he then put into an urn – along with a note explaining what he had done and just enough cash to pay for his funeral!

*   *   *

Shortly after the end of the Second World War, Herman Wallischauser and his family who lived in Hechingen, near Stuttgart, were delighted to start receiving food parcels from some relatives in America.

In a country starved of virtually everything, these parcels were a lifeline and always opened with the greatest excitement. In one such delivery, in January 1947, Frau

Wallischauser found a tin containing a fine grey powder which she assumed was instant soup.

However, when mixed with water, the soup seemed rather weak, and so the good lady added a little semolina from the same food parcel. Nonetheless, the family ate the dish with relish – declaring it to be the best soup they had ever tasted.

The following morning a letter arrived for the Wallischausers from their relatives in America. It hoped the family would enjoy the latest despatch of food, and added that included with the parcels they would find a small tin.

This, said the letter, contained the ashes of their dead grandmother – who had asked for her remains to be returned to Germany for scattering on her native soil . . .

At the funeral of the famous Hollywood film star, Humphrey Bogart, in 1957, his widow, Lauren Bacall, surprised mourners by having a whistle placed in the urn containing his ashes.

Explained Miss Bacall later, 'It's because of what I said to him in the first film we made together, "To Have and Have Not" (1943) – If you need anything, just whistle!'

*   *   *

The funeral of Anna Bochinsky was going according to plan in the village of Moinesti in Rumania, in the spring of 1959. The coffin, with its lid open as is customary in the country, was just about to be lowered into the

ground, when suddenly the 'corpse' sat bolt upright.

The mourners stood rooted to the spot in dumb astonishment as the woman then jumped from her coffin and without a word ran quickly away.

They were even more horrified when Anna ran out of the cemetery, across the road, and was killed by a passing motor car.

*　　*　　*

There is a story told in Newcastle about an old woman who was standing outside a Bingo hall waiting for it to open, when a funeral procession suddenly went by.

At this, the old lady broke away from the queue, crossed the road to

the hearse, and carefully placed a red rose on the coffin.

When she rejoined the queue, there were several kind remarks passed by those standing alongside her.

'My, what a beautiful thing to do,' said one.

'Eee, not many folks would do that these days,' said another.

And a third added, 'That was a lovely thought, hinney.'

'Oh, well,' said the woman after a moment's pause, 'it was the least I could do for him – he was a good husband to me.'

* * *

A lucky escape turned into a fatal mistake for Arthur McAlisdair while

he was watching a funeral procession in San Diego, California, in May 1960. For in order to get a better view of the proceedings, he tried to run across the road in front of the hearse and was knocked over.

Though he was not hurt, Arthur was immediately urged by an onlooker to lie still and feign injury so that he could claim compensation.

Unfortunately, as he did so, the driver of the hearse leapt from his vehicle to see that his victim was all right – leaving his handbrake off in his haste – and the big vehicle rolled forward, crushing Arthur to death.

*　　*　　*

At the close of a funeral in Cape Town, South Africa, in June 1965, a

mourner was just about to leave the graveside, when she realised that her small floral hat had fallen from her head.

Anxiously, the woman looked around the spot where she had been standing, for she planned to wear the hat to a cocktail party later in the day. But there was no sign of it.

Later, a shamefaced undertaker confessed he had mistaken the hat for a floral tribute and buried it with the coffin!

* * *

Aware that he was dying of lung cancer, retired university teacher, Dr James Beckford of Glendale, California, decided to have his body frozen in liquid nitrogen so that it

might be restored when a cure for the dreaded disease had been found.

After the doctor's death, aged 73, in January 1967, three members of the Cryonics Society lead by Dr Dante Brunel carried out his wishes by freezing the body prior to it being transported to Phoenix, Arizona, for storing.

Explained Mr Raymond Vest of the Cryonics Society, 'It took eight hours to freeze the body. The doctor's widow was present, as was his son, Norman. We had to send Norman out for more ice once.'

*   *   *

In order to prepare herself for mourning at the funeral of her father, a former snake charmer who lived in

New Dehli, India, 23-year-old Suva
Mohotti spent the night before the
ceremony carefully washing her long
hair and piling it up into a bun on her
head.

But as she stood by the graveside
the next day, she suddenly collapsed
and died. A doctor who inspected
Suva's body found a bite mark on her
neck and diagnosed that a small
poisonous snake must have coiled up
in her bun during the night.

*   *   *

Returning to his home in Latheron
after a research trip in the mountains
of eastern Scotland, botanist Mr
Fergus Wick was confronted by the
sight of a coffin being brought out of
the house and placed in a hearse.

Horrified that either his wife or daughter had died during his absence, Mr Wick rushed up to the group of mourners. After a moment's stunned silence, he was greeted by hysterical shrieks.

The mourners – who included his wife and daughter – were convinced that it was *he* who was dead and lying in the coffin!

It was later explained that a body had been found floating in a nearby lake and had been identified by both Mrs Wick and her daughter – as well as two family friends and the local dentist – as that of Mr Wick.

After he had inspected the body in the coffin, Fergus Wick said, 'It doesn't look anything like me – but I am glad to be alive!'

*   *   *

A practical joker in California named Martin Olsen conspired with two of his friends in 1971 to make the day of his funeral – when it eventually arrived – an explosive one.

He made arrangements that after his death, his body was to be taken to a Los Angeles mortuary and there placed in a coffin stuffed with fireworks.

Explained Martin, 'I want to go out with a big bang when they cremate me.'

* * *

Printed in the order of service for the funeral of Mr Daniel Patrick Murphy of Brooklyn, New York, in February 1971, were the following words:

'To relieve the monotony of sitting, while the coffin is removed for transportation to the cemetery, mourners are asked to rise during the singing of the chorus, "Fix'd in His everlasting seat".'

*　　*　　*

Actor and writer, Jeremy Lloyd, revealed in 1973 that he was leaving the most unusual instructions for his funeral.

'I am always very depressed by graveyards,' he told the *Sunday Express* in October of that year. 'So whatever is left in my bank account I want used to buy a hillside with a cave in it and, wearing my velvet jacket, I want to be put sitting on a chair gazing out of the entrance.

'I think there are one or two fairly cheap caves in the Highlands,' he added.

*   *   *

It was no ordinary funeral when they buried Ferdnand Bachelard, the 'Biggest Man in the World', at Rocourt, a Belgian village near the border with France, on 6 January 1976.

Aged 53, 7ft 9ins tall and weighing a massive 42 stone, Ferdnand died from heart failure during an operation, after years of performing in circuses all over the globe as 'The Atlas Giant'.

It took twelve bearers to carry his huge coffin from the village church to the cemetery. His giant's grave had

taken two grave-diggers three days to complete, and filling it in required another twelve hours' work.

His tombstone, though, was just 12 inches tall!

*   *   *

It was the kind of interruption to startle anyone. But as the priest was saying the final prayers over the open grave of 52-year-old Picu Aymaran, at Chaobomba in Bolivia, the lid of the coffin was thrown back and the good lady scrambled out!

Although Picu had been confirmed dead by two doctors *before* the funeral, she was clearly still alive – and had a bizarre story to tell her amazed relatives.

'I was in Heaven and saw the Glory of the Lord,' she claimed. 'It was perfect bliss, the colours were indescribably brilliant. I had a feeling of weightlessness.

'Then all of a sudden a voice told me to go back to Earth,' she added.

*   *   *

Sixty-six-year-old Henry Taylor was one of four pall-bearers at a funeral in Kensal Green Cemetery in London, in 1977. The coffin the men were carrying was known to be lined with lead and consequently required particular care as it was manoeuvred down a narrow path to the grave.

Just as the quartet neared the grave, however, the four men were

required to execute a neat reverse of half a dozen steps. Though well used to such turns, Henry Taylor unfortunately stumbled and fell.

Unable to hang on to the heavy coffin without support at all its corners, the other three men let go . . . and it fell on to Henry, fatally injuring him.

*   *   *

After the funeral service for a close friend in January 1978, two men in Thonburi, Thailand began to argue about the mysteries of life and death. When they then started to dispute the problem of the chicken and the egg and which came first, the argument turned to blows and one man tragically killed the other.

The dead man had maintained it was the egg.

*   *   *

After conducting a funeral service for a well-known local drunkard, Arthur Mage, in December 1978, the Revd James Owen of Cambridge received a number of complaints from parishioners.

'One is never surprised at the lack of charity that exists,' he said of the service which was attended by members of the police force, the local Publicans' Association and Alcoholics Anonymous.

A memorial address was also given by Dr Michael Avon who said, 'Arthur was born to suffer. Often he was mugged for the money it had

72

taken him days to beg.

'It is true that he was a homeless alcoholic who made well over a hundred appearances before the bench,' added Dr Avon. 'However, he once gave me the most perfect definition of the Christian life – unfortunately it was some years ago and I have lost the piece of paper on which I jotted it down.'

*　　　*　　　*

There was a surprise in store for Mrs Christine Jay when she arrived for a funeral at Studland near Swanage in Dorset, in June 1979. For she had travelled all the way from her home in Montreal, Canada with her husband, for the funeral of her grandmother –

only to find the old lady was still alive.

'We were quite surprised to find Granny Dade up and about,' said Mrs Jay.

The old lady herself explained what had happened.

'Most people only meet at funerals nowadays,' said Granny Dade. 'Therefore I decided to have my "end-of-term" party while I was still active. In the end so many people turned up we had to hire the village hall!'

*   *   *

There are lots of stories of bizarre instructions left by people about the disposal of their ashes. Tony Gribble of Bristol, for instance, said that he

wanted his remains to be used as the
family's egg-timer 'so that I shall
continue to be of use after death',
while horse racing enthusiast Jack
Greenslade of Berkshire asked for his
ashes to be scattered on the winning
line at Ascot where he had not missed
a meeting in forty years, 'so that I can
watch the winners go by'.

Then there was Ted Haynes, the
landlord of the Harbour Tavern in
Newhaven, Sussex, who asked for the
urn containing his ashes to be placed
behind the bar; while an old
American submariner, Hiram Cassidy
of Louisiana asked for his remains to
rest in the deep – shot from the
torpedo tube of his boat, the
Barracuda.

But perhaps the most amusing
story of all concerns wealthy oil lamp
manufacturer, Sydney Sherwood, who
prided himself on the tidiness of his
works in Birmingham. His
instructions were that his ashes were

to be scattered over the workshop floor, 'because of my affection for the place'.

They didn't remain there for long, though – because just as in life, the place was neatly swept up again shortly afterwards!

*　　*　　*

On the morning of 28 July 1980, a number of family relatives gathered in the home of Mrs Joan Carson of Lake Kushaugua in New York State. They had come to pay their last respects to the lady who had been certified dead from heart disease.

As they gazed at the open coffin, however, Mrs Carson suddenly sat up and gazed wonderingly about her.

And at this, her daughter dropped dead from fright.

A funeral service which it had been hoped would help reconcile two branches of the Methodist Church in Africa went somewhat wrong in August 1981.

As Mr J. J. Matote, the Member of Parliament for Cofimvoba, in the Transkei, was reading a funeral oration for his friend, Mr H. Gwenshe, he suddenly produced a pistol from his pocket.

Mourners looked on in some alarm as Mr Matote continued, 'I will fire this in honour of my dead friend.'

He then pulled the trigger and shot the officiating clergyman, the Revd V. Nyobole, in the leg.

At this, the service ended in disarray and Mr Matote was charged with attempted murder.

*　　　*　　　*

The strangest funeral on record took place in October 1982 in the United Arab Emirates, according to a report in the *Khaleej Times*.

Over fifty mourners attended the service which was accompanied by prayer and songs. The chief mourner was also the person most directly involved with the bereavement.

For the ceremony was to mark the 'death' of one of the man's legs – severed in an accident – prior to its burial in a specially built tomb!

*   *   *

The bad luck associated with the number thirteen came true yet again in China, in 1983.

On the morning of Friday 13 May, a group of thirteen people were struck

and killed by a number 13 train while crossing a railway track in District 13 of Peking.

They were all members of the same family, too – and on their way to a funeral!

*   *   *

The American playwright Tennessee Williams (1912–83) lived a controversial and often bizarre life. But the strangest event of all he reserved until his death.

In his will, Williams asked to be cremated and then have his ashes scattered in the Gulf of Mexico at the exact spot where his favourite poet, Hart Crane, committed suicide by jumping from a ferry.

Williams explained his request in these words, 'I never met Crane – but this will be my chance!'

*   *   *

The funeral procession for the famous screen Tarzan, Johnny Weissmuller, in Acapulco in January 1984, was staged in typical Hollywood style and attended by several thousand fans.

'We arranged for an ape to lead the procession, walking beside the coffin and with his hand upon it,' explained one of the organisers, Mrs June Views. 'Then, as Johnny was laid to rest, twenty loud-speakers rang out with his famous jungle-cry!'

*   *   *

It was a funeral the like of which the dour Yorkshire town of Bradford had never seen before. It happened on 26 January 1984, when 62-year-old Billy Ellison, known locally as 'Chief Lame Fox' and 'The Best Indian in Town' was given a Sioux funeral!

Billy's coffin was draped with a bearskin and decorated with a traditional Indian head-dress and pipes of peace.

Several of the mourners were actually dressed as Indians – and a ceremonial dance finally saw the old chief off to the happy hunting grounds in the sky.

*   *   *

Relatives who had paid to have the ashes of their dear departed scattered

from a plane over the Pacific Ocean
or on the peaks of the Sierra Nevada
mountains, were distressed to
discover in June 1984 that they had
actually been dumped in a field
outside San Francisco.

The relatives who first uncovered
the fraud, planned to sue the pilot for
emotional damage. But theirs was
nothing like the problem faced by the
local police.

For reports indicated that the
dump of ashes, representing as many
as 9,000 people, was up to a foot
deep. And the police were unsure as
to whether they could charge the pilot
under a law which forbids 'the
co-mingling of human remains'.

*   *   *

Taxidermist Neil Dewhurst of Bridgnorth, Shropshire, who has worked on everything from alligators to a two-headed lamb, was amazed when a caller in September 1984 asked him, 'Please stuff my grandad.'

The woman told Neil that she and her family did not want to bury their much loved old grandfather – but have him stuffed and dressed in his military uniform to stand in the hall!

'The enquiry was unbelievable,' said Neil later, 'but I'm sure the woman meant it. I had to refuse, though, because I thought it might be illegal.'

*   *   *

An American, Ken McAvoy, of Fort Lauderdale, offered in September

1984 to take messages to the other side after his funeral.

Expecting to die within four months because of a brain tumour, McAvoy advertised in a south Florida magazine to deliver messages from the living to their departed relatives at $50 a time.

Said McAvoy, 'My mission, when I make the transition into the other world, is to help others. Upon my death, I will be brain dead, then cremated, and the message goes with me. That's the best way I can explain it.

'Take my word for it,' he added, 'I'm guaranteeing I'll find people whether there are 25 or 2,500. I *will* follow through.'

*　　　*　　　*

A vast, palatial mausoleum was
erected in Jammu, the winter capital
of Kashmir, in November 1984, as a
memorial to a victim of Sikh
extremists.

The killing had touched off
widespread protests and the
mausoleum was erected by militant
Hindus.

It contained only the head of the
victim . . . a cow.

*   *   *

A funny thing happened to a London
merchant banker, Mark Murphy, on
his way to a funeral along the M4 in
June 1985.

As he drove along, he spotted two
hitch-hikers beside the motorway and,
with time to spare before the service,

decided to pull over to give the pair a lift. Much to his surprise, Mark discovered the two men were comedian Billy Connolly and singer Rod Stewart.

The entertainers told Murphy that they had been forced to thumb a lift after Rod Stewart lent his Mercedes to members of his family, like him en route for Heathrow, whose van had broken down.

Mark was so amazed, that he asked for the pair's autographs 'in case the other funeral guests thought I had been hallucinating', he said later.

And his reward for this kindness? Minutes later, Mark Murphy was stopped by the police for driving – in great confusion – on the motorway's hard shoulder!

*   *   *

86

The deepest memorial service on record must surely be that for Dr Oliver Lloyd which was held 500 feet underground at Swildon's Hole, near Priddy, Somerset, in August 1985.

Several dozen friends gathered in the subterranean vault to honour pathologist Dr Lloyd, who had died the previous year aged 73. While alive, he had regularly held birthday parties in the same place!

*　　*　　*

The winning letter in a 'Laugh – I Could Have Died!' competition organised by the *Sunday Mirror*, in October 1985, for readers' most embarrassing moments was this entry from Mrs R. Stanton of Chester:

'Jumping off a train I saw several members of a family about to get on. "Oh!" I enthused, "a happy family gathering. How lovely."

'"Actually," came the reply, "we're just going to bury my mother."'

* * *

The ultimate prize was announced for anyone scoring a hole-in-one at the eighth hole in the New South Wales PGA Tournament, in Australia, in November 1985. The sum of $10,000 in cash or . . . a lavish funeral complete with ornamental tombstone.

If a play-off was needed to decide the winner, the organisers added, the eighth hole would – appropriately – be used as the sudden death hole!

Things went fatally wrong for a group of French mourners keeping a midnight vigil around the coffin of a 97-year-old neighbour who had died on 12 December 1985 at Villeparisis, to the south-east of Paris.

The mourners, all in their eighties, were found dead alongside the coffin the following morning – they were asphyxiated by the fumes of a defective gas heater put on to keep them warm.

*   *   *

It was only at his funeral that eccentric Eric Camp got what he had wanted for most of his life – to be treated as a woman.

For when 82-year-old Eric was buried in January 1986, he was

dressed as a woman in his coffin, and during the funeral service at Baldock, Hertfordshire, he was also referred to by the vicar as 'she'.

It was not until he was 77 that Eric decided to become a woman – but doctors then told him he was too old for a sex change operation. So the 6-foot pensioner lived the last years of his life as 'Marion' wearing make-up and dresses.

His coffin also bore the inscription, 'Marion'.

*   *   *

Eccentric farmer, Vasser Rowe, of Clavering in Essex hated funerals – especially slow-moving cortèges. So he demanded a speedy, stylish send-off when his time came, and that was

exactly what his life-long friend the local undertaker, Alan Peasgood, gave him in January 1986.

For during the six-mile journey from Clavering to the chapel of rest in Saffron Walden, Mr Peasgood put his foot down in his hearse and at one point reached the far from funereal speed of sixty-seven miles per hour!

'I'm just sorry I didn't make it to seventy,' Mr Peasgood said afterwards. 'But I'm sure Vasser would have approved. He was a great character and not a man to dawdle. And it *was* seven miles above the speed limit for the winding country roads!'

*   *   *

Mrs Evangeline Riterman of Chicago, USA became so angry listening to a preacher conducting the funeral service of a distinguished local citizen on her television, in February 1986, that she picked up the set in her sixth-floor apartment and hurled it to the floor where it exploded.

That was the unhappy lady's explanation when she was later charged with manslaughter because of a death caused by the fire which followed.

*　　*　　*

The Americans have come up with a bizarre new form of burial, it was announced recently in *The Mortician's Journal*.

The aim is to reduce the body mass without cremation. First, the corpse is

cooled by liquid nitrogen to −100 degrees Centigrade which makes all the body tissue rock solid. Then the frozen body is pulverised by an automatic hammer until all the chunks of bone, head, etc. do not exceed half an inch in size.

Lastly, the particles are reduced to 5 per cent of their original weight by 'freeze drying' which takes out all body fluids.

What is left, the *Journal* adds, 'can be stored in an urn for burial or domestic storage'.

*　　　*　　　*

It will be the ultimate funeral – your ashes despatched into space in a tiny gold-coloured capsule that will remain suspended 1,900 miles above

the Earth for 63 million years.

For an estimated cost of $3,900 per capsule, The Celestis Group of Florida, USA plans to launch the first such 'last resting place in orbit' in 1987.

Talking about the plans for these 'space mausoleums' in 1985, a spokesman said, 'With this method, the remains will never be disturbed again – it's not like having to put up with a road going through a cemetery.

'Future mourners will be able to send the sacred remains of their loved ones into undisturbed rest in the sterile, eternal and inviolable space with the stars, planets, Moon and Sun as their markers.

'I'm sure it will be seen by many people as an improvement on scattering ashes on their gardens or on a favourite golf course. It destroys the grass, you know,' he added.

III

GRAVE PLACES
Cemetery Stories

In order to prove whether there was life after death or not, naval officer Ben Wangford, an agnostic, requested to be buried in Watford Parish Church with a fig in his hand. If there should be an afterlife, he said, then the fig would germinate in the coffin and burst the tomb.

Several years after his funeral in 1800, the officer's tomb *did* split open and a healthy fig tree appeared.

*   *   *

Body-snatcher Peter Harkan came to an unhappy end in Meath Cemetery, Scotland, in 1823. With two young assistants, he broke into the graveyard one midnight and was just about to remove a corpse when disturbed by a night-watchman.

The two assistants were rather fleeter of foot than Harkan, and had already cleared the cemetery wall when he arrived panting and almost out of breath. Halfway over, his hands were grabbed by the two men. At that same moment, the watchman also arrived and grabbed Harkan's dangling legs.

In the ensuing struggle, both sides pulled so vigorously that the body-snatcher soon joined the ranks of those he had plundered!

*　　　*　　　*

One of the most curious monuments
to be erected in a cemetery can be
found in the little town of Canden, in
Maine, USA.

It is a marble statue some 28 feet
high which towers over the tomb of
Captain Hanson Gregory who died in
1847.

The statue was raised on the
centenary of Captain Gregory's birth
to commemorate his great
achievement . . . making the hole in
the doughnut!

*   *   *

The story of the travelling coffin is
one of the most unusual cases of
burial on record.

In 1899, the famous actor Charles
Francis Coghlan was buried in a

cemetery at Galveston, Texas very close to the shore. On 8 September 1900 a West Indian hurricane swept the Gulf Coast of America, and a torrential flood deluged the Galveston cemetery, uncovering and carrying out to sea a number of coffins – including that of Charles Coghlan.

When the hurricane subsided and the tragedy in the cemetery was revealed, no one expected to see any of the coffins again.

But fate had other plans in store. For several months later, after evidently being carried by the Gulf Stream for almost 1,500 miles, the coffin was washed ashore at the appropriately named Fortune Bridge on Prince Edward Island in Canada – the very spot where Coghlan had been born seventy years previously!

*   *   *

Matthew Burnett, a grave-digger in Coventry during the first two decades of this century, was famous for his wit which was in marked contrast to his gloomy appearance.

A much repeated story is told of a mean local businessman who, after Burnett had buried his wife, tried to get him to lower his fee.

For some time the two men haggled, with Burnett quite unwilling to drop his price for a man he knew was well able to afford it. Finally, the grave-digger lost his patience and glaring at the businessman, pointed in the direction of the grave and shouted:

'Either pay me my due – or up she comes!'

It is said the man paid in some haste!

Not surprisingly, the night before her husband's funeral, Mrs Josephine Anderson of Leadville, in Colorado, found it difficult to sleep.

Despairing of getting any rest, she finally got up, dressed and went for a walk on the night of 30 September 1902.

According to a later report she entered the local cemetery where a grave had already been dug for her husband's coffin. And in the darkness she must have slipped and fallen, for she was found dead at the bottom of the 15-foot shaft the next morning.

*   *   *

The most appropriate name on a tombstone anywhere in the world is to

be found in the picturesque Mount Hope Cemetery, at Rochester, near New York. It marks the last resting place of:

WELCOME A. SOULE

*   *   *

An advertisement from the *London Gazette* of 12 November 1946.

FOR SALE. Gas fire. Hardly used. Simulated flames. A bargain at £10. Contact: Enfield Crematorium.

*   *   *

Forever in the shadow of death was a certain American miner named J. R. Wilson of Salt Lake City, whose memorial stone erected on his death in 1948 reads:

J. R. WILSON
worked the
GRAVEYARD SHIFT
in the
COFFIN MINE
at the head of
DEAD MAN'S GULCH
near
TOMBSTONE FLAT
in the
FUNERAL RANGE
25 miles from
POISON SPRINGS
in
DEATH VALLEY

Happily, Mr Wilson only died of old age!

    *   *   *

Even the occupants of graveyards are entitled to a vote in Russia, it seems.

During the infamous rule of Joe Stalin, an election return in 1947 from one of the districts of Moscow gave him more than 100 per cent of the votes!

The count showed that he had achieved 2,122 votes in a constituency of only 1,617 people.

It later transpired that Stalin's over-zealous supporters had added the roll-call of the local cemetery into the total!

*　　　*　　　*

Extract from a letter to the *West Sussex County Times* of June 1949:

'I write on behalf of the churchwardens of St Mary's Church

to state we think it desirable to make
a change in the arrangements for
keeping the grass in the cemetery in
order, as Mr Brazly is now getting
very infirm. We have given him notice
to expire at Christmas.'

*   *   *

Antonio Satanassi, the grave-digger of
Riofreddo, near Cesena, in southern
Italy, was busy digging a new grave
on the morning of 17 June 1955, when
the earth beneath his feet suddenly
crumbled and he fell into the hole. So
loose was the soil, that it buried the
poor man up to his head.

For some time, Antonio called for
help, but according to a local
newspaper report, 'No one would
come near thinking he was a ghost.'

When, finally, two men *did* pluck up courage and approach the grave and saw the helpless grave-digger, he had lost consciousness. He was then dug out and taken home, where the first impression was that he must be dead.

At this a priest was called and was in the process of giving Antonio the last rites when – again according to the newspaper – 'the corpse of the grave-digger regained consciousness and scattered all the mourners by his loud imprecations against the excessive superstition of the local population!'

*　　　*　　　*

Jim Stanley had thought it might be a bad day from the time he got up on 4

November 1961. First, the alarm had failed to go off to wake him early to get to an important business meeting. Then, a toaster in the family home in Queensland, Australia had caught fire and delayed him further.

The last straw for Jim was when his car failed to start. Although his wife, June, could not drive he asked her to take the wheel while he gave the vehicle a push.

Starting suddenly, the car took off with Mrs Stanley clinging grimly to the wheel. Despite her lack of skill, she managed to pass over twenty other cars, before careering helplessly into a wall.

Jim Stanley, arriving on the scene shortly afterwards, found his poor wife dead and his car a write-off. The wall she had struck was that of a cemetery.

*   *   *

French businessman Henri Bidard became famous in 1963 for sleeping each night in his garden in a coffin!

Said Henri from his home in Argentan, 'After we die, most of us are destined to spend the rest of eternity inside a coffin. I wanted to get accustomed to being inside one *before* I die.'

*　　*　　*

Perhaps the weirdest case of coincidence on record was that reported in America, in 1969.

Miles Lucas was driving home from New York to his home in New Jersey when his car was suddenly struck by another vehicle. Miles was slammed against the door and fell out on to the road.

His driverless car then continued to weave along the road until it finally crashed through a wall and came to a stop just beyond.

The wall was, in fact, that of a cemetery, and when the uninjured Miles Lucas arrived to inspect the damage to his car he found it had come to rest against a tombstone bearing the name . . . Miles Lucas!

Statisticians believe the odds against something like that happening are 6,250,000-to-one!

*　　　*　　　*

While clearing an area of the Sand Springs Cemetery in Oklahoma, in January 1973, graveyard worker Charlie Hufford discovered what looked like a human hand.

Only *looked* like a human hand, for though it had five fingers, human-like nails and was flesh coloured, there was fur on it and webbing between the fingers.

A local doctor declared it to be . . . a duck's foot!

*　　*　　*

'The lonely ghost' made a cemetery at Lariano, in central Italy, something of a tourist attraction in December 1973. In fact, the parish priest, Father Don Mantani, found that only a handful of people attended his services, while hundreds congregated outside the cemetery to see the ghost.

According to reports, there was only one ghost in the cemetery

because it had only been open a
month and contained just one grave –
that of Eva Candidi, wife of a local
bar keeper.

Scores of people reported seeing a
figure in black struggling to get out of
the tomb after the cemetery gates
were closed at night.

Said cemetery keeper, Alberto
Galante, 'Some people come from
their homes after supper and stand
outside the cemetery for hours –
sometimes until dawn – hoping to see
the ghost.

'The other night when I passed by
on my bicycle just before midnight,
there were about 1,000 people peering
through the railings. I think the ghost
is lonely, and until her coffin is joined
by others her spirit will seek to
escape.'

*   *   *

Topless American dancer, Frenchie
Renee, claimed a new world record by
being buried alive in a coffin for a
month in December 1974 – in
company with the four rattlesnakes
and a boa constrictor she normally
used in her act.

Emerging from her tomb, the exotic
dancer from San Francisco drank a
glass of champagne and said, 'The
burial was the only way I could get a
vacation!'

*   *   *

The Society for Perpendicular
Interment announced in Melbourne,
Australia, in June 1976, a worldwide
campaign to have dead people buried
upright in cylindrical cardboard
coffins.

An official spokesman of the society said in a press statement, 'This is the only way to solve one of our most pressing problems. Horizontal burial just takes up too much room in our overcrowded world.'

*　　　*　　　*

A decomposed human arm complete with a hand which was found in a cemetery in Falmouth, Cornwall, in December 1976, had a message attached to it which read:

'In case you need a hand . . .'

*　　　*　　　*

It was a curious and recurring dream that disturbed the sleep of Maria Mattei at her home in Rome. For twelve years, in fact, she kept dreaming that she could hear the voice of her dead daughter pleading to be fetched from the coffin in which she had been buried at 2 years old.

Finally, in May 1977, Maria could bear the dreams no longer and told her parish priest. With his help, permission was obtained to open the tiny coffin and put the distraught housewife's mind at rest.

But on opening the grave, the mystery only deepened. For though the child had obviously been dead all those years, the body looked as if it had only been buried the day before.

*　　*　　*

You can hear voices from the grave in America – literally.

In August 1977, a new gimmick in the burial business was announced in the form of the talking tombstone. When mourners got near enough to the grave it automatically synthesised a message such as:

'Hi, there! I was Jane Smith. I died in 1976 on 16 June at 12.05 pm. Thanks for coming to visit me – and have a good day!'

Explaining how the tombstones worked through a speaker connected to a concealed photoelectric cell, a spokesman of the manufacturers, Creative Tombstones, said: 'With our computerised system people feel their loved ones are still with them.'

*　　*　　*

114

As a Mrs Elizabeth Grumpin was praying quietly at the graveside of her sister, Mary, in a New York cemetery in October 1977, the tombstone inexplicably toppled over and trapped her beneath. Though not badly injured, it was still some time before her plaintive cries were heard by other visitors to the cemetery and she was rescued.

Later, during a court case brought against the municipal authorities by the woman's husband, Mr Jim Grumpin, he said, 'It took five hours to get my wife free. I found the incident upsetting because my wife's nephew was crushed to death by a similar gravestone two years ago!'

*　　　*　　　*

There were unexpected developments when Mr Maywe Ndango, a Zambian taxi-driver, picked up Mrs Yona Kikko in the town of Jerrah, in March 1978.

Tragically, the lady collapsed and died in the taxi – and though Mr Ndango later sought repayment from the widower, Mr Brubar Kikko, this was resisted on the grounds that his charges were above and beyond the agreed fare for the destination to which Mrs Kikko had been travelling.

Mr Ndango thereupon issued an action against Mr Kikko explaining, 'The inconvenience of driving to the nearest cemetery justified the increased fare.'

*   *   *

116

The military tattoo being put on by the US Army troops based in West Berlin, in July 1978, was intended to be a rare spectacle for the thousands of onlookers.

Called 'Patriotism Is Life', the event was highlighted by a solo parachute jump by Sergeant George McGraw waving a huge Stars and Stripes flag.

Unfortunately, as the Sergeant fell his parachute lines became entangled with the flag and he plunged to his death amidst the tombstones in an adjoining cemetery.

* * *

Widow Mrs Beatrice Dingle of Providence, Rhode Island announced

in August 1978 that she was suing the local Archbishop, Rodney Towler, because for seventeen years she had continuously been praying and leaving flowers at the *wrong* grave.

She explained, 'I thought my husband lay beside Rear Admiral Cloker. But when Mrs Cloker died it was revealed that there was in fact *no* coffin in the spot adjacent to the Admiral's.

'I have spent thousands of hours on my knees and almost $2,000 on flowers – all at the wrong place. It was wasted time and I blame the Archbishop!'

*　　　*　　　*

A little piece of graveyard history was made in Tulsa, USA in February

1980, when a Mrs Skip Switzer asked
for her mother to be the first person to
be buried in a *pet cemetery*.

She explained, 'We approached the
owners of Pawprint Memorial Turf
and asked if they would mind mother
lying beside "Rinty" her German
shepherd dog. They said she could –
so we bought the plot and made a
miniaturised effigy of mother holding
"Rinty's" lead which now stands
beside the dog's effigy.

'This makes good family sense,'
added Mrs Switzer, 'and we have all
decided to share the same resting
place when the time comes – each, of
course, with our own effigy.'

*   *   *

The occupant of a local cemetery was declared the winner of an election in Texas, in November 1982.

The unhappy loser of the poll was a Republican politician, J. Everett Ware, who was defeated in the election for the South Central Texas District. It was revealed after the count that the winner was Democratic Senator Wilson . . . who had been dead for six weeks!

*　　　*　　　*

Alexander Richter of Pennsylvania, USA held a unique record in the annals of burial grounds. For every week for sixty years he placed a wreath on his *own* grave!

As a young man in the twenties, Richter travelled a lot, and after an

absence of several years, he returned home to find that the body of a man who had been drowned had been mistaken for him and laid to rest in the family plot reserved for him!

* * *

The Chinese couple had just been married – but as the report in the *Peking Daily* of 6 January 1983 put it, 'Death could not part them.' For the pair were both dead and attended the service in their coffins!

Although everything else about the macabre ceremony in Shandong Province was as usual – a priest, lots of guests, piles of presents and a marriage feast – the honeymoon was a return to the graveyard.

The 'ghost marriage' had been arranged by the bride's influential parents after she had been killed in an accident – to prevent her suffering the dishonour of being a spinster in the afterlife.

A matchmaker had been employed by the parents to find a suitable husband – and he came up with an unmarried young man who had died a few weeks earlier.

For the ceremony, both bodies were exhumed – and then afterwards returned together to the husband's tomb while the guests stood by 'eating sweets and burning money and clothing as offerings to the couple', according to the *Peking Daily*.

*   *   *

The tomb of Lenin in the mausoleum in Red Square, Moscow, is certainly the best known and most visited tomb behind the Iron Curtain.

Year in and year out, millions of Russians as well as visitors from the West, troop through the gloomy building for a glimpse of the body which is kept in a specially refrigerated glass coffin. It is usually a cold and rather unemotional experience.

But not for one British tourist, in 1984, when there were apparently some problems with the freezing system.

For as the man passed the coffin he was amazed to see a movement . . . and V. I. Lenin's right ear dropped off!

*   *   *

When London company director Paul Ashton ordered a message in Hebrew to go on his mother's gravestone in July 1984 he did not get quite what he asked for. It was only one word that the stonemason got wrong, but it made all the difference to the sentiments.

It was the rabbi who told a horrified Paul what had happened – for instead of the inscription reading, 'She goes happily into the next world', the gravestone read, 'She hiccups into next world.'

*   *   *

The buxom American singer Dolly Parton confessed in an interview in July 1984 that she got the inspiration

for some of her most haunting
melodies while wandering around
graveyards!

'They're the one place I can be
assured of a bit of peace and quiet,'
she was quoted as saying.

*   *   *

The case of the subversive tombstone
is unique in cemetery history. For in
September 1984, Tan Chu Boon of
Singapore was found guilty of erecting
a memorial which 'tended to advocate
acts prejudicial to the Republic's
security'.

The tombstone was placed on the
grave of Tan's brother, Chay Wa,
who had been executed in Malaysia
the previous year for communist
underground activities.

The government prosecutor told the court that the inscription glorified Chay Wa by describing him as a revolutionary warrior and a martyr. It also contained other inflammatory terms aimed at overthrowing the governments of Singapore and Malaysia – where communism is outlawed – by violent means, the prosecutor said.

Tan was sentenced to a year in jail (though this was later reduced to a month) and the black marble tombstone officially branded 'a subversive document' – though it still stands to this day!

*   *   *

It was not the kind of sight a graveyard worker usually expected to find in a cemetery – a woman sprawled across a tomb crying, 'Ah, found you at last!'

The bizarre sight occurred in November 1984 at Carisbrooke Cemetery on the Isle of Wight, and the person the worker found apparently talking to the dead was an authoress, Beryl Bainbridge.

Beryl was in fact researching a book about the Revd John Selby Watson who murdered his wife in 1871.

'It had taken me four years to find his grave,' said Beryl, 'but it was so embarrassing. I was just so pleased to find it that I fell on the gravestone without a thought that anyone might be looking!'

* * *

To 'celebrate' twenty years in business, the Scunthorpe Municipal Crematorium held an open day in November 1984.

According to reports, three guides took relays of visitors on forty-minute conducted tours against a background of piped music by Richard Clayderman.

Reported one journalist, 'Before the visitors examined the bone crushers and ovens normally heated to 1,000°F, which take seventy-five minutes to burn an average-size corpse, they were given an explanatory leaflet.'

And Mrs Betty Martin, chairman of the council health committee, said, 'People are curious about what happens in a crematorium and we have been able to allay their fears by showing them. Everyone was delighted by what they saw.'

About 2,000 people attended the open day.

There was an unfortunate choice of words in the announcement for a contest to find contemporary designs for cemeteries which was sponsored by the Memorial Advisory Bureau in February 1985.

Outlining the idea of the contest, the Bureau said that the main objective was to 'liven up the appearance of graveyards'!

*   *   *

It was probably the strangest plan ever to come before the Greater London Council, according to a report in the *Daily Mirror* of 11 November 1984.

Alternative funerals was the idea – or 'memorial celebrations' as they

were to be called – in cemeteries reserved for *Women Only*!

*   *   *

If you have a macabre sense of humour (and you surely *must* have to have read this book) imagine finding your final resting place in the cemeteries of any of these little towns and villages.

In Britain we have: Bubney Moor, Bushy Ruff, Cutty Stubbs, Cool Pilate, Bumper Castle, Thick Withins, Glutton Grange, Butchersick, Dirty Gutter, and Lloyds Nightsafe.

But all pale into comparison with these from America: Midnight (Mississippi), The Boneyard

(Arizona), Skull (Nebraska), Skeleton (Oklahoma), Frankenstein (Missouri), Hanging Limb (Tennessee), Bad Axe (Michigan), Cut and Shoot (Houston), Stab (Kentucky), Razor (Texas), Hemlock (Indiana) and – if you can believe it – Transylvania (Virginia) and Bloodsucker Lake in Saskatchewan!

*　　　*　　　*

DEATH'S DOOR

This inscription was put on the grave of William Death, a forebear of the author, who died in Wandsworth, London in 1879.

He was not, though, an undertaker, but a . . . stonemason!

Also by Richard De'ath

DIED LAUGHING

How often have you said 'I nearly died laughing'?
Incredible as it may seem, in March 1975 someone
actually did! Alexander Mitchell collapsed and
died after laughing non-stop for half an hour at his
favourite television comedy programme.

Even on their death beds, some people manage to
retain their sense of humour. Sir Noel Coward
departed this life with the words 'Goodnight my
darlings, I'll see you tomorrow.' Some last words
are inadvertently humorous — as the audience
chuckled at the end of his act, Tommy Cooper
ad-libbed 'I thought it would get a bigger laugh
than that.' It was the last joke he ever made.

This hilarious collection of last moments from all
the corners of the globe proves that even in death
there can, on occasions, be a touch of humour.

LAST WILL AND TESTAMENT

'I give unto my wife my second best bed, with the furniture'

Shakespeare's will reveals both his wit and perhaps a streak of malice. Spouses — of either sex — often suffer in the will of their late lamented loved ones within these pages. The widow who received

'five hundred pounds. But she is only to come into the enjoyment of it after her death in order that she may be buried suitably as my widow'

had cause to feel aggrieved.

Last Will and Testament includes a host of wills where the beneficiaries received a lot less than they bargained for, as well as some very odd bequests indeed.

TOMBSTONE HUMOUR

Here lies the body of Andrew Gear,
Whose mouth did stretch from ear to ear;
Stranger, step lightly o'er his head,
For if he gapes, by Josh, you're dead!

This stone was raised to Sarah Ford
Not Sarah's virtues to record
For they're well known by all the town
No, Lord, it was raised to keep her down.

Bizarre, hilarious and unusual epitaphs are to be found throughout chuchyards around the world. Here gathered together in one place are the tributes people pay themselves and their 'loved' ones.

TRIAL & ERROR

The law is not usually cause for a laugh. This collection of human weakness shows another side to lawyers and the law. There's the clerk who stole from his employer and asked if (in the event of his arrest) the solicitor would defend him; a case of bigamy involving six wives; a burglar who felt aggrieved at being identified by a man who kept his head under the bedclothes — and many more.

LAST LAUGHS
Russell Ash

Irritating neighbours and fond husbands, hot-blooded housewives and religious maidens, intrepid cavalrymen and Rosa the cow — all are commemorated in *Last Laughs*, a rambling collection of epitaphs from four continents and four centuries. Bill Tidy's original cartoons add a hilarious dimension to the sentiment, wit, absurdity or plain ill-humour of our forefather's final remarks to their passing fellow men and women.

NEWS FROM A SQUARE WORLD
Royston Jeans and Alan Kamin

'The international literary group writers for peace gathered in Cologne, West Germany, in meetings that saw plans for peace interspersed with shouting matches and fistfights for control of the podium'

'Richard Spates and Teresa Thames fell for each other in a big way. They exchanged wedding vows during a 45-second free-fall from a plane over Lakewood, New Jersey. Jumping with them were the Minister, 10 wedding guests and two photographers'

Just two of the true stories taken from a wide range of reports from around an apparently square world!

THINGS YOU DIDN'T KNOW YOU DIDN'T KNOW!
Graeme Donald

Tuxedo

Son of a Gun

Gazumping

Flushing Toilets and Thomas Crapper

Hobson's Choice

In Hock

The fascinating stories about the origins of these—and many more—common expressions. This book tells you all you need to know!

THINGS YOU THOUGHT
YOU THOUGHT YOU KNEW!
Graeme Donald

If there is one thing more fun than learning it is finding out that your teachers are wrong. From deflating the ego of the ever present pub bore to infuriating the self-appointed experts who tell us what is what, this book will arm you with an arsenal of amazing facts to enable you to shoot holes in the myth-taken beliefs that people have been swallowing for years. So the next time someone tells you that heat rises, that punks have Mohican hair-dos, or that Cook discovered Australia, either make a bet or tell them to go out and buy this book.

Also by Richard De'ath

Died Laughing	£1.75 ☐
Last Will and Testament	£1.50 ☐
Tombstone Humour	£1.50 ☐
Trial and Error: or Beyond the Legal Limit	£1.75 ☐

Also in Unwin Paperbacks

Gourmet Sex *Tony Pinchuck*	£1.95 ☐
Last Laughs *Russell Ash*	£1.50 ☐
News from a Square World *Royston Jeans & Alan Kamin*	£1.95 ☐
Things You Didn't Know You Didn't Know! *Graeme Donald*	£1.95 ☐
Things You Thought You Thought You Knew! *Graeme Donald*	£1.95 ☐

All these books are available at your local bookshop or newsagent, or can be ordered direct by post. Just tick the titles you want and fill in the form below.

Name ....

Address ....

....

....

Write to Unwin Cash Sales, PO Box 11, Falmouth, Cornwall TR10 9EN.

Please enclose remittance to the value of the cover price plus:

UK: 55p for the first book plus 22p for the second book, thereafter 14p for each additional book ordered to a maximum charge of £1.75.

BFPO and EIRE: 55p for the first book plus 22p for the second book and 14p for the next 7 books and thereafter 8p per book.

OVERSEAS: £1.00 for the first book plus 25p per copy for each additional book.

Unwin Paperbacks reserve the right to show new retail prices on covers, which may differ from those previously advertised in the text or elsewhere. Postage rates are also subject to revision.